Original title:
Murmurs of the Moss

Copyright © 2025 Creative Arts Management OÜ
All rights reserved.

Author: Zachary Prescott
ISBN HARDBACK: 978-1-80567-357-6
ISBN PAPERBACK: 978-1-80567-656-0

Tales Told by Thickets

In the thicket, a fox wears a hat,
Chatting with birds about this and that.
Squirrels gossip of acorns lost,
While rabbits calculate their hopping cost.

The foliage chuckles at a joke told low,
As the raccoon dances, putting on a show.
Ferns wave politely, quite suave and neat,
While the toad croaks rhythms with tapping feet.

Soft Songs of the Subsoil

Deep below, the worms hold a band,
Playing tunes with a rock as the stand.
Mice come to listen, tails in a curl,
And a mole offers snacks from his underground pearl.

They harmonize sweetly, a catchy beat,
Toadstools sway gently, tapping their feet.
The roots find it funny, a sight to behold,
As they root for the songsters, brave and bold.

The Quietude of Clandestine Roots

Beneath the ground, secrets unfold,
Roots tell the stories from ages of old.
A shy little beetle, with a grin so wide,
Joins the conspiracy, a true friend and guide.

With whispers they plot to tickle the trees,
Causing laughter in whispers with mischievous tease.
The fables of soil drift up with a laugh,
As the daisies giggle, forming a staff.

Rustling Reveries in Green

In the greenery, a debate ensues,
Is it better to bask or dance in the dews?
The shrubs take a vote, while twigs intertwine,
Looking for sunlight, under which they shine.

They argue with petals, all colors around,
As the daisies declare, 'We're the best in the ground!'
With laughter and rustles, the afternoon fades,
In a tapestry woven of leafy charades.

Echoing Footfalls Among the Foliage

A squirrel slips on a pinecone,
As branches start to sway.
The birds above all giggle,
And shout, "Hey, watch your way!"

A hedgehog rolls like thunder,
Unruly in its path.
The leaves just shake their heads,
Stifling their leafy laugh.

A rabbit hops in circles,
Chasing its own tail,
While shadows dance around it,
In this odd, leafy tale.

The forest holds its secrets,
With laughter in the air.
Even the tallest trees sway,
In their own funny flair.

The Patina of Ancient Earth

Old oaks wear moss like jackets,
   Their bark a bit askew.
  A chipmunk with a top hat,
  Says, "What's a lad to do?"

  A snail drags its slow body,
    In its own sticky spree.
  It waves at passing breezes,
"Hi there! Care to trot with me?"

The stones, they keep on talking,
  About things they can't digest.
"We've seen it all, dear creatures,
  But standing still's our best!"

With laughter and with wisdom,
  The earth just rolls her eyes.
  In the dance of silly moments,
   Nature's humor never dies.

Cradles of Sylvan Serenity

A leafy bed for dreaming,
Where creatures snore in peace.
A badger hums a tune loud,
Which causes quite the crease.

The ferns are twisted gigglers,
They tickle with their fronds.
A turtle plays the violin,
While butterflies respond.

In soft and green embraces,
The moon casts playful light.
A family of raccoons,
Is holding a snack fight.

With berries flying high,
And laughter all around,
The cradles rock to rhythm,
Of joy they have found.

The Harmony of Hidden Realms

In shadows of the thicket,
A chorus starts to play.
The frogs sing opera nightly,
"Oh, what a grand display!"

Mice hold tiny parties,
With cheese upon a plate.
They dance to rustling rhythms,
With moves that fascinate.

The mushrooms wear their colors,
Like outfits for a ball.
And beetles, proud and swanky,
Are zipping down the hall.

With laughter in the undergrowth,
Every critter knows,
There's humor in the wild side,
Where silliness just grows.

Murky Dreamscapes of the Meadow

In a field where shadows play,
The daisies giggle, come what may.
A worm does waltz beneath the grass,
While ants host parties in a glass.

A frog in slippers, hops around,
In search of snacks on soggy ground.
The clouds are sheep, they drift and snore,
While sunbeams tickle, wanting more.

A ladybug in shades of red,
Debates the flowers on who's best fed.
And caterpillars dance a jig,
While butterflies leap, oh so big!

By dusk, the crickets start a band,
A symphony played with stout demands.
The moon joins in, on flutes of light,
As creatures laugh into the night.

The Subtle Movements of the Mould

In corners dark where fungi thrive,
A party sprouts, do not deprive.
With every spore, a tiny cheer,
The mold brigade is bringing beer.

They throw their hats made out of fluff,
To celebrate their squishy stuff.
A snail taps toes upon the ground,
As mushrooms sway, the fun profound.

The mildew throws a cheese soiree,
Where rats in tuxedos come to play.
The dust bunnies start to swing and sway,
As everyone's invited, hip hooray!

But careful now, don't make a fuss,
For in this scene, it's those who cuss.
The cobwebs spin a tale of woe,
While spiders eye the dance floor show.

Ephemeral Echoes of the Earth

Down in the soil, whispers dwell,
A gopher shares its funny tale.
With roots a-twisted, meet and greet,
The radishes tap their tiny feet.

The stones all gossip, can't you hear?
As worms recite their verses clear.
They roll their eyes and laugh at ants,
Who always seem to lose their pants.

The daisies chuckle at the breeze,
Who juggles pollen with such ease.
A beetle struts, its pride on show,
While grasshoppers leap to steal the flow.

The earthworms wiggle in delight,
As echoes of the day take flight.
With all this whimsy underground,
You'll find the best jokes all around.

Nature's Minuet of Green

In woodlands dense where laughter grows,
A squirrel dances on its toes.
The trees all clap with leaves of cheer,
As bushes giggle, "Come in here!"

The critters gather, take a stance,
While mushrooms call, "Let's have a dance!"
With twirls and skips, they share the fun,
A minuet beneath the sun.

The hedgehogs wear their spikey hats,
And play a game of hide and spats.
A porcupine tries to do ballet,
And tumbles down, much to their dismay.

But laughter echoes through the glade,
And friendships blossom, never fade.
With every heartbeat of the green,
The merry tunes keep us serene.

Unearthed Secrets of the Underbrush

In the green beneath, secrets sway,
Tiny critters have much to say.
A worm named Larry starts a debate,
While ants complain about their weight.

A beetle boasts of his shiny shell,
While mushrooms gossip, do tell, do tell!
The roots are tangled, a jumbled mess,
But in their chaos, they find success.

A snail with speed, or so he thinks,
Claims he's the fastest, quick like a wink.
While quicksilver breezes just rush on by,
He takes his time, and waves goodbye!

Oh, the sly fox makes a quick joke,
About the trees and their ancient yoke.
As laughter echoes through the trees,
Who knew the ground held such a tease?

The Enigma of Earth's Embrace

Digging deep, we find quite a show,
With critters conspiring, scheming below.
A rogue earthworm hosts a wild party,
With dancing roots, it gets rather hearty.

The mushrooms play loud music at night,
While crickets join in with sheer delight.
The soil has secrets, and they know best,
To keep their antics well-concealed at rest.

A dog's nose twitches, he tries to pry,
While the gophers giggle and wonder why.
With each little poke, they scatter and flee,
You'd think they'd learned from a squirrel's decree!

But under the ferns, tales keep alive,
Of mischief and giggles, in the hive.
So dip your toes where the earth meets the air,
Join in the laughter, if you dare!

The Hidden Heartbeat of the Wilderness

A squirrel stands guard with a serious face,
While a raccoon plots a food-finding race.
The trees chuckle, swaying so free,
While beneath their shade, ants sip tea.

In hollows and nooks, echoes ignite,
Whispers of wisdom, oh what a sight!
A wise old owl gives a wink and a nod,
As he listens to gossip drawn from the sod.

The sneaky hedgehog rolls in a ball,
Shouting complaints that nobody can haul.
"Oh, why's it so prickly?" he gives a scowl,
While laughter erupts in the trees and the fowl.

A turtle named Slow likes to take bets,
On who'll eat what through the leafy sets.
And in the wild, every critter knows,
Laughter is love in the forest, it grows!

The Gentle Dance of Dappled Sunlight

Sunbeams play hopscotch on leaves overhead,
While the flowers rejoice, their faces widespread.
A bumblebee buzzes, a comedian proud,
As a ladybug squints in her red polka crowd.

In shady spots, lizards strut,
With poses so grand, oh what a cut!
They flaunt their scales, a sight to behold,
While the sun laughs bright, shimmering gold.

An old toad croaks, "Why'd the fly cross the road?"
It's a question that lightens the load.
As beetles chuckle and ladybugs chuck,
The sun gets brighter, drawing good luck!

Even the shadows dance in delight,
In a waltzing ballet, oh what a sight!
With flowers and critters under the beams,
Nature's a performer, or so it seems!

Awakened Dreams of the Earth

In the carpet of green, a gnome's head peeks,
A wig made of weeds, oh, how it squeaks!
Tangled in roots, he's lost in a dance,
Wiggling his toes, he gives fate a chance.

A squirrel jogs past, with a nut in tow,
Chasing its tail, moving fast like a pro.
The earthworms hold parties, underground fun,
While daisies gossip, lighting up the sun.

Glittering wishes float over the ground,
As petals spin tales that make laughter resound.
In the shadows, a rabbit puts on a show,
With hops that impress, quite the star of the row.

The whispers of soil, tickling the air,
Tell stories of mischief with flair and a glare.
It's a carnival scene, oh, what a display,
Where laughter and nature blend into play.

Low Murmurs Beneath Starlit Boughs

Crickets compose, an orchestra at night,
Their tunes fill the dark, oh, what a delight!
A raccoon in pajamas, quite snug in a tree,
Offers snacks to the stars, as happy as can be.

Fireflies twinkle, igniting their glow,
Sharing secrets with leaves, putting on a show.
An owl's perplexed, his spectacles askew,
Debating the wisdom of one wisdom or two.

Mice in tiny tuxedos, dancing on leaves,
Slip and slide gracefully, among glimmering thieves.
They toast acorn cups, in style, and with glee,
As night unfolds laughter in the arms of the trees.

The moon laughs quietly, with beams full of light,
Watching the frolic, it swells with delight.
Under the boughs, where mirth sits on the throne,
The woodland party goes on, never alone.

The Soft Heartbeat of the Green Realm

In a meadow of chuckles, the dandelions sway,
While grasshoppers flirt, in a chirpy ballet.
A spider spins tales that hang like a laugh,
Crafting webs of wonder in a delicate staff.

Butterflies gossip with colors so bright,
About flowers in bloom, and quite the sight.
A turtle in shades naps under a hat,
Dreaming of races he often thinks at.

The breeze joins the fun, wearing a smile,
As it rustles the leaves, playing with style.
Two bees in a frenzy, buzzing a tune,
Invite the whole grove to dance under the moon.

Under so much laughter, the roots start to sway,
Unseen little critters join in on the play.
As giggles grow louder, it's clear, oh so sweet,
The green realm's alive with a joyful heartbeat.

Sotto Voce Among the Statuesque Trees

Trees whisper quietly, with stories galore,
Of squirrels dressed lavishly, moonlit encore.
A raccoon in a cloak struts off with a pie,
Ripping through stardust while wishing to fly.

Amidst the old trunks, a snail holds a feast,
Grazing on lettuce, a culinary beast.
Beneath the tall shadows, laughter takes root,
Charming little critters, in their leafy suit.

Woodpeckers tap-tap, creating a beat,
As frogs join in rhythm, tapping their feet.
An owl rolls its eyes, too wise to engage,
In the raucous adventures that spring from each page.

Yet laughter echoes softly, through branches so high,
Where every leaf wiggles, and breezes comply.
It's a secretive party for those who can hear,
The whispers of nature, a gathering near.

The Soft Echo of the Evergreens

In the woods where squirrels play,
Trees gossip in a funny way.
Whispers float on breezy smiles,
As I trip over roots for miles.

A wise old pine told me a joke,
Said the fir laughed till it almost broke.
Bark beetles dance in merry glee,
While moss winks at a bumblebee.

Nuts drop down like clumsy pranks,
Evergreens chuckle at the swanks.
They shake their limbs, oh what a sight,
Nature's laugh under dappled light.

Branches stretch and stretch some more,
Sharing secrets from the forest floor.
Laughter drips like dew on me,
While squirrels joke in harmony.

Murky Melodies of the Mossland

In shadowed nooks where sunlight dims,
Frogs croak out their serenade hymns.
Mossy carpets, soft to the toes,
Hide the giggles, no one knows.

Toads tell tales of their great quests,
While mushrooms wear their funkiest vests.
The logs chuckle, they've seen it all,
As the crickets give a chorus call.

A snail slips by with a wobbly grin,
Sassy in the slippery din.
Worms twirl under the moisture's spell,
Charming the soil with stories to tell.

In the murk, a dance commences,
With frogs and slugs in vast pretenses.
Nature's humor wraps us tight,
In this land of green delight.

The Chants of the Canopied Depths

Up above, the branches sway,
Birds sing out in a raucous display.
Raccoons juggle acorns with flair,
While shadows mime without a care.

Beneath the leaves a secret band,
Shimm'ring roots do a goofy stand.
Whispers tumble like a fruit-filled pie,
As raccoons snicker and pass me by.

Sunbeams tickle the laughing clover,
Frogs play tag, taking each other over.
Bumblebees buzz with silly grace,
In a dappled, wooded race.

A twig snaps, and chaos ensues,
Amidst the trees, in quirky hues.
Nature sings a joyful tune,
Made of laughter, sun, and moon.

Sighs of the Saturated Soil

Beneath the ground where roots entwine,
Earthworms giggle at their own design.
Dress shoes sink in the muddy play,
As puddles pop in a clownish way.

The toiling ground hums a jolly tune,
In the garden, where the weeds attune.
Potato plants wear hats of mud,
While carrots boast of their crunchy flood.

A turnip squawks in bubbly glee,
Saying, "Look at me, I'm lunch, you see!"
Laughter sprinkles through the dark,
In a soil patch with a hidden spark.

Pickles pry with a crooked grin,
Under rain, they dance and spin.
In this earth, all woes are small,
As laughter echoes beneath it all.

Glistening Drops of Forest Lore

In the woods where secrets hide,
A squirrel falls, and he's quite spry.
He shakes off dew like a shower,
And giggles at his acorn pie.

The ferns dance lightly in the breeze,
Pinecones gossip with the trees.
A fox trips over a hidden root,
Wishing for less clumsy shoes, if you please!

In the sunlight, the critters prance,
To an unheard tune, they all dance.
A rabbit sneezes, and chaos ensues,
You'd laugh too, if you had half a chance!

Underneath the leafy cloak,
A toad croaks like a wise old bloke.
With tales of dreams and grime-filled nights,
While beetles dance and giggle at the joke.

Rustic Rhythms of Hidden Paths

Down the trail, there's mischief afloat,
A turtle in a tiny boat.
He paddles slow, with utmost pride,
While a rabbit whizzes by with a farting note!

The mushrooms squabble, who will be lunch?
They argue loud, in a singing bunch.
A bear strolls by, without a care,
Sniffing for snacks in a berry crunch.

Each pebble whispers, each twig replies,
To squirrels plotting the greatest prize.
But oh, that crow with the beady eye,
He laughs as their plans turn to flies!

So wander here, where oddballs roam,
Amidst the trees, you'll find a gnome.
In every rustle and every cheer,
Lies the charm of this peculiar home.

The Veil of Verdure

Behind the leaves, there's chatter bright,
A bear trying to dance, what a sight!
He stumbles on vines and shimmies around,
While crickets play tunes in delight.

The willow weeps for a silly reason,
It lost a bet to a tiny seasoned.
A million tiny raindrops applaud the scene,
Making plans for a joyous treason.

A hedgehog, dressed in sheer delight,
Wears a flower crown, oh what a fright!
He turns to pose for his dreamy fans,
And trips over roots that hide from sight.

So sway along the shady lanes,
Where giggles burst from leafy plains.
In all this laughter, joy will grow,
As nature's whimsy lightly reigns.

Secrets in the Shady Abode

In the nook where the sunlight fades,
A chubby raccoon makes his raids.
He thought he found a treasure chest,
But it's just an old shoe, oh the charades!

The loons in the pond are quite the crew,
Quacking secrets they must pursue.
They splash around, causing a scene,
As frogs join in with a boisterous moo!

The leaves above are having a blast,
Telling tales of the days that passed.
A Lazy Lizard, king of the term,
Drinks sun tea, slow and steadfast.

Find here the laughter in shade so sweet,
Where woodland chatter and jiggles meet.
In this wild haven, let joy abide,
And leave behind the world's repeat.

Whispers Beneath the Canopy

Squirrels gossip about the nuts,
While butterflies gossip of their guts.
Fungi giggle in the soft, cool earth,
Tickling the toes of trees since their birth.

A rabbit tells tales of carrot hunts,
With flowers snickering, all in good fun.
The breeze joins in with a wily tease,
Cupping the leaves like a childhood breeze.

Crickets croon a silly old song,
While ants march by, thinking they're strong.
During the night, they form a parade,
Dancing in shadows, their moves will not fade.

Under the stars, a raccoon rolls,
Breaking the silence with comical trolls.
Under the laughter of twilight's embrace,
Nature's humor is all over the place.

Secrets of the Woodland Floor

The squirrels have secrets they won't confess,
Hiding acorns in a game of finesse.
Tangled roots twist like old fishing lines,
While the mushrooms hold court, in their funny designs.

Twitching tails and rustling leaves,
The grassy knolls join up and weave.
Wombats roll by, with cheeks full of greens,
Claiming the prize of the forest's cuisine.

With each little step, the ground can giggle,
As rabbits hop close, doing a wiggle.
The songbirds chirp in a comedic choir,
To forecast a rain, they wholly conspire.

Under the brush, the grasshoppers leap,
Joining a contest of who can sleep.
The dance of the critters, a woodland delight,
Bringing smiles to creatures, even in twilight.

Echoes in the Leafy Shade

In the shade where the shadows stretch out,
There's a ruckus of critters, no room for doubt.
The chipmunks trade quips with a quick little jibe,
That leaves all the frogs just to laugh and to vibe.

The wind sends a tickle through tall, green hair,
As plants roll their eyes, too cool to care.
A hedgehog high-fives a wobbly snail,
Both dreaming of winning a slow-motion trail.

Treetops whisper secrets, a playful refrain,
About ants with big plans in a miniature train.
Raccoons gather around in a marshmallow feast,
Sharing their tales, outdone by the least.

With fireflies flicking like tiny lanterns bright,
The woodland giggles, alive in the night.
No worries or woes, just the joy of the cheer,
In this leafy domain, life's a laugh every year.

The Lullaby of the Fern

In a cozy nook where the ferns like to play,
Little shadows bounce, making giggles all day.
Fronds sway gently to a soft, silly tune,
While crickets choreograph under the moon.

The woodland's a stage, with creatures so bold,
Telling tales that never grow old.
A hedgehog in spectacles reads from a book,
While toads clap their hands, and owls come to look.

Beneath the fern's shade, all worries take flight,
As nature spins yarns in the soft, dark night.
The babbling brook joins in the fun,
Creating a song that never is done.

So here's to the laughter in the forest's embrace,
Where every leaf dances, in a whimsical space.
With smiles that linger like morning dew,
The secrets in nature are funny and true.

Nature's Silent Symphony

In the forest, a squirrel sneezes,
While the cat stalks, trying to tease us.
The leaves laugh, they shimmer bright,
As crickets dance in the pale moonlight.

A frog croaks, a bit off key,
With a flair that's pure comedy.
The owls hoot their nightly jokes,
While raccoons plot to steal our smokes.

The wind whispers tales of yore,
Of critters planning the next great score.
The bugs take notes, but what a fuss!
Life's an act on this green bus!

So if you hear a rustling sound,
Know that laughter's all around.
The trees chuckle, their branches sway,
In this playful musical ballet.

Cradle of the Ancient Grove

In the shade of trees so grand,
A gopher practices his bandstand.
The roots tap dance beneath the ground,
While the chipmunks erupt in a sound.

The old tree trunks wear such a grin,
For every acorn is a win!
The wise owls roll their eyes and wink,
As they find comedy in our clink.

A hedgehog wears a tiny hat,
While a sloth debates where he's at.
The ferns whisper with a giggle,
As the mushrooms break into a wiggle.

Underneath the starry stage,
Nature's book writes every page.
With laughter shared in every nook,
The forest thrives on each funny hook.

Veiled Whispers in the Twilight

The shadows play a game of peek,
As raccoons plan their nightly tweak.
The moon grins wide, what a sight,
As fireflies dance, oh what a fright!

A rabbit hops into a snag,
While the stars twinkle, 'No need to brag!'
The pines rustle, and crickets strum,
Their symphony makes us feel numb.

Beneath the glow, a fox tells tales,
Of mischief that never fails.
Each echo carries a tale so grand,
Of slippery things that can't withstand.

Laughter floats on the evening breeze,
As bats swoop with utmost tease.
In the quiet twilight's light,
Nature giggles with pure delight.

Eldritch Chants Beneath the Oaks

Beneath the boughs, the squirrels plot,
With acorns that they've carefully caught.
A badger winks, as if in on jokes,
While the owls roll their eyes at folks.

The mossy floor is a stage set,
For frogs and toads, a fine duet.
Their back-and-forth, oh such a riot,
Turns a quiet night into a diet.

The ancient trees lean in for more,
As giggles echo through their core.
With quips and laughs written in bark,
Every creature plays their part in the dark.

So listen close to the woodland lore,
Where laughter opens every door.
Nature's whims, a comedy show,
In the oak's embrace, let the humor flow.

Wistful Whispers in the Wilderness

In shadows deep where critters play,
The laughter drips from skies of gray.
A squirrel chats, a raccoon sings,
While bouncing beetles have their flings.

The trees all sway in playful jest,
As pinecones cast their heads on quests.
The leaves point fingers, giggle free,
At ants who march like them, you see!

A frog hops in with croaks so bold,
Telling tales of nights of old.
Grasshoppers join the chorus light,
As fireflies waltz in pure delight.

Oh, nature's stage, a grand parade,
With creatures weirdly masquerade.
In every rustle, every breeze,
The forest's charm will always please.

The Talking Treetops

High above where sparrows dart,
The canopies share tales from the heart.
The branches stretch with whispers spry,
While clouds float past with a cheeky sigh.

A crow confesses love to a kite,
While owls chuckle deep in the night.
A woodpecker drums a silly tune,
Rattling branches beneath the moon.

The willows sway with graceful flair,
Making dreadful puns in the air.
As dandelions blow their seeds,
They snicker at the buzzing beads.

Each rustling leaf shares jokes anew,
A comedy show just for a few.
Nature's laughter fills the expanse,
In this leafy, lively dance.

Lullabies of the Leaf

In verdant beds where shadows rest,
The leaflets sing, they know the best.
With giggles soft they lull the breeze,
And rustle tales among the trees.

A drowsy hedgehog snores away,
While acorns tease the bright sun's ray.
A butterfly with winks so sly,
Sips nectar dreams as time drifts by.

The night unfolds with twinkling lights,
As critters make whimsical sights.
With whispers low, the branches sway,
In this dreamy leaf ballet.

Chirping crickets hum a tune,
As sleepy frogs croon to the moon.
In nature's arms, all giggles cease,
For even leaves need moments of peace.

Beneath the Burgeoning Boughs

Under branches, life's a joke,
As rabbits hop and hedgehogs poke.
The daisies dance, the tulips sway,
In sunny patches where we play.

A lizard struts, a master's pose,
While woodlice tickle cactus toes.
The butterflies pairing like horses,
Two pals laughing on their courses.

The trees conspire, a secret fun,
With shadows stretching, hide and run.
Each twig a friend in games of chase,
As squirrels giggle, keeping pace.

So join the round of leafy cheer,
Where every rustle means good cheer.
Together bright, we weave the day,
In nature's wild and wondrous play.

Secrets of the Silent Grove

In a hollow log, a squirrel pranced,
He practiced dance moves, but glanced askance.
A snail popped by with a helmet so bright,
Claiming he's ready to join in the fight.

The tree frogs croaked a curious tune,
Under the light of a rickety moon.
A raccoon chuckled, his paws full of jam,
Said, "Join the feast, it's a tree party slam!"

A whispering breeze made the branches sway,
While beetles held court and the ants danced away.
They filled the air with giggles and cheers,
As nature's creatures brushed off their fears.

So next time you wander, listen real close,
To tales of a snail and a dancing oak dose.
For secrets are hidden where laughter will bloom,
In the shadows where critters dispel all their gloom.

The Lullaby of Lichen

A chubby little toad sung a silly song,
As lichen nodded, all fuzzy and strong.
The mushrooms giggled, their caps in a spin,
Saying, "Toad, you're crazy! Let the fun begin!"

A worm in a tuxedo slithered with flair,
Claiming he'd dance on a branch without care.
But the winds joined in with a puff and a gust,
Sending him tumbling, oh what a bust!

The moss on the ground chuckled right back,
As a family of beetles formed a gold track.
They rolled in the dirt like they just won a prize,
While ants cheered them on, with sparkly eyes.

So if you're weary from the day's heavy grind,
Hitch a ride on a breeze and leave worries behind.
Beneath the moon's glow with the stars on parade,
Nature sings lullabies that never will fade.

Echoes in the Underbrush

In the thick of the woods, where the shadows do creep,
A raccoon dined gently, on pizza he'd keep.
But a startled bird squawked, flapping wildly away,
Only to trip on a twig – "What a way to play!"

A hedgehog complained 'bout his cousin the mouse,
"Why'd he bring crackers to the forest to rouse?"
But the laughter grew louder from their leafy stage,
As all of the forest turned to a rage.

With laughter and echoes, the night came alive,
A dance of the critters, oh how they'd thrive.
The ferns were applauding, giving all they could,
In the bustling underbrush, where all seemed good.

So during your stroll through the thickets and haze,
Know laughter can lighten the heaviest days.
For hidden behind every leafy brush hum,
Are creatures with stories that tickle and strum.

Shadows of the Verdant Veil

A fox in the shadows wore glasses so thick,
Claiming he read every tale with a flick.
Yet when he turned pages, oh what a blunder,
The stories went flying like a storm of thunder.

A lazy old turtle snoozed by a creek,
Dreaming of truffles so rare and unique.
But woke with a start as a chipmunk ran by,
"Oh dear, I've just lost my latest supply!"

The trees whispered secrets with rustling leaves,
As bugs in a choir hummed songs for the thieves.
While mischievous mice played tag in the night,
Tangled in shadows, oh what a funny sight!

So tangle yourself lightly in nature's delight,
And join in the laughter that sparkles so bright.
For shadows can hold the best tales of all,
With quirky surprises at every leaf's fall.

Where the Spirits of the Moss Dwell

In a patch of green where shadows play,
The giggles of faeries dance all day.
Toads wear hats, frogs sing songs,
While trees sway gently, all night long.

Squirrels debate over acorn stew,
Bunnies wear ties, oh what a view!
They tiptoe around in their little shoes,
Chasing the wind, spreading the news.

Goblins sneak snacks with crafty grins,
Trading secrets, playing their sins.
Every leaf whispers a silly joke,
As the sun filters through, a warm cloak.

So if you wander and hear a cheer,
Know there's mischief waiting near.
Join the laughter, grab a dance,
In this lively realm, take a chance.

The Quietude of Roots and Stones

Under the ground where the oddities creep,
The stones have gossip, but it's theirs to keep.
Roots waltz freely, a jolly parade,
Tickling the toes of those who invade.

A snail pulls a prank on a sleeping lizard,
Waking him up with a very loud gizzard.
They chuckle together, rolling on moss,
Creating a ruckus they deem as a boss.

Old mossy rocks host a comedy night,
Jokes about shadows and the absence of light.
Crickets laugh, so loud and bright,
Joining the fun till the end of the night.

So next time you sit on a boulder's throne,
Listen closely, you're not alone.
The quietude hums with laughter and cheer,
In this world of quirks, all is clear.

Echoes of Time in the Forest Depths.

In the depths of the woods, where time runs slow,
An owl plays chess with a curious crow.
The rocks hold history, some juicy and grand,
While vines reenact all the tales they've planned.

Beneath the ferns, a turtle's got style,
Rocking a hat with a dapper smile.
Mice hold debates, who's fastest they prance,
Avoiding the cat with a sly little dance.

The echoes of laughter bounce off the trees,
Rabbits trade carrots for humorous keys.
They unlock the night with stories so bold,
Revealing the secrets that never grow old.

So wander these depths if you crave a good laugh,
You'll find quite the crowd beneath each sweet gaff.
Time here is funny, a playful jest,
In the forest's embrace, you'll feel truly blessed.

Whispers Beneath the Canopy

Underneath leaves where secrets unfold,
The whispers of mischief are silently bold.
Squirrels swap tales about nuts they once stole,
While foxes play poker beside a bright hole.

The canopy rustles, a giggly parade,
As raccoons declare a hilarious charade.
They juggle with acorns, a sight to behold,
And laugh at the sun, so bright and so cold.

Bubbles of laughter rise from the ground,
As mushrooms conspire to spin tales around.
They plot a grand feast for the bugs in the night,
Over pudding and pie, everything feels right.

So take a stroll under branches so wide,
Where shadows and giggles become your guide.
Beneath the green dome, the humor is free,
In nature's embrace, join the jubilant spree.

The Hidden Chorus of the Glade

In the forest, critters sing,
A squirrel strums on a twig,
The rabbits tap dance quick,
As frogs croak, the beat's big.

Leaves rustle, as if to cheer,
The dance floor's gleaming bright,
With antlers bumping left and right,
They party until the night.

Acorns roll like marbles too,
All the fawns join in the fun,
With little hiccups and sway,
They jig till the day is done.

Nature's laughter fills the air,
A concert that's free for all,
So grab your friends and have a share,
When woodland critters call.

The Soft Descent of Shade

Beneath the canopy of green,
A snail rides a leaf like a boat,
He shimmies and slides, what a scene!
Holding tight, he starts to float.

The shadows giggle, stretch, and yawn,
As drowsy moths begin to glide,
They swoosh, they spin, they laugh at dawn,
In a blanket of leaves, they hide.

Wanderers wander, hoping to peek,
At this comedy of nature's show,
With every step, they hear the squeak,
As mushrooms sprout with quite a glow.

Each blade of grass has its own joke,
A ticklish air begins to rise,
As lizards chuckle, tails are stroked,
In this playful paradise.

Wistful Whispers Underfoot

Beneath our feet, there's chatter bright,
With ladybugs dressed in polka dots,
They gossip in notions, pure delight,
Sharing tales of the newest spots.

The lost socks dance in secret glee,
While worms wiggle and twirl with cheer,
What wise advice from roots, you see,
In the soil, their whispers are clear.

Grasshoppers play a chess match bold,
As crickets snap their fingers too,
Each leaf has secrets to be told,
In laughter soft, the day feels new.

When night falls with winks of stars,
The bugs hum joyful, buzzing tunes,
As shadows giggle, free from bars,
In the dark, the night's a boon.

The Silent Serenade of Shadows

Underneath the tall, proud trees,
The fireflies wink, a glowing crew,
They clap their hands, a gentle tease,
While shadows spin and leap anew.

Night owls joke with moonlit beams,
Each quip ignites the silken air,
With whispers woven into dreams,
As crickets join the midnight fair.

A tortoise in a top hat winks,
While mice wear ties, it's quite a ball,
In shadows' glow, everyone thinks,
That giggles are the best of all.

So join the fun, let laughter lead,
In this night where plays unfold,
The shadows' dance and silly creed,
In nature's mystery, be bold!

Beneath the Shade's Embrace

In the gloom where shadows play,
A squirrel spins tales of the day.
He juggles acorns with great delight,
While mushrooms giggle, a funny sight.

The trees are snickering at the ants,
Who waltz with joy in their tiny pants.
A beetle boogies, round and round,
While laughter echoes from the ground.

In the twilight, whispers take flight,
As fireflies dance in the fading light.
Frogs croak jokes in a ribbiting tone,
While night wraps us in a chuckle of its own.

And under laughter's sprawling tree,
We listen to nature's comedy.
With every rustle and every pause,
Life is a giggle, just because.

The Soft Pulse of Nature's Heart

There's a ticklish breeze in the air,
As flowers sway with flamboyant flair.
A rabbit hops in a pair of shoes,
While daisies gossip, sharing the news.

The clouds all gather for a chat,
Big and fluffy, silly as a cat.
A punchline bursts from a distant tree,
Leaves chuckle softly, can't you see?

In the underbrush, the tick tock sounds,
Of busy critters scampering around.
Nature's pulse beats a quirky tune,
While the moon cracks jokes to the sleepy raccoon.

So let's dance in circles, round we go,
With critters and laughter stealing the show.
Underneath the starry, twinkling chart,
Lives the funny pulse of nature's heart.

Whispers in the Wildwood

The forest giggles, what a tease,
As branches sway in the playful breeze.
A fox in glasses reads a book,
While brambles chuckle at every nook.

The owls hoot wisdom, quirky and spry,
While butterflies flutter with a wink, oh my!
A bear juggles berries, round and sweet,
While bumblebees buzz to the drum of their beat.

The sunlight tiptoes on the ground,
While the crickets play the funniest sound.
Mice giggle softly, tippy-toe,
As the wildwood dances and puts on a show.

With every whisper, a joke unfolds,
As nature's humor in layers molds.
Under these whispers, life's a riot,
In the wildwood's heart, let's start a riot!

Forgotten Lyrics of Mossy Stones

On ancient stones where mosses bloom,
Forgotten lyrics chase away gloom.
A nutty squirrel sings off-key,
While stones chuckle, oh what a spree!

In the shade where funny tales grow,
A tortoise dances, moving slow.
With every step, he cracks a grin,
As the moss nods with a cheeky spin.

The flowers hum a silly song,
While beetles tap dance all day long.
A ladybug joins the maracas beat,
While stones watch on, feeling the heat.

In the quiet cool of nature's dome,
We laugh with the stones, we're finally home.
With every chuckle, each joyful tone,
Life's forgotten lyrics are ours alone.

The Tones of the Tangled Trail

In the woods where giggles play,
Trees gossip in a leafy ballet.
Squirrels dance with nuts in tow,
While silly shadows steal the show.

Frogs wear crowns of morning dew,
Hopping madly in a queue.
A raccoon stumbles, trips on a stay,
And nature laughs at clumsy sway.

Leaves rustle, tickled by a breeze,
Whispers shared among the trees.
A chipmunk's tale, a laughter crash,
Echoes through the lush green mash.

In this playful, leafy maze,
Nature's jesters entertain with praise.
So when you wander, listen close,
To the giggles that the woods can boast.

The Muffled Messages of the Glade

In a glade where secrets hide,
Buzzing bugs and frogs collide.
A butterfly with winks of flair,
Whispers jokes beyond compare.

A snail races, slow but steady,
While cheeky birds chip in, "Are you ready?"
Trees chuckle at the weather's mood,
As flowers sway, distinctly rude.

The breeze carries tales from the brook,
Where minnows play, and fish forsook.
A toad croaks out a pun so fine,
Leaving all the crickets in a line.

Laughter blooms, it spreads like light,
In this glade, all feels just right.
So join the fun, let worries cease,
For nature's joke is pure release.

Reverberations of the Rooted Realm

Oh, the roots that stretch and twist,
In a dance that none could resist.
A badger's antics, a funny sight,
Digging holes with all its might.

Gnarled branches wave hello,
As critters plot a funny show.
A hedgehog snickers, rolling round,
In this realm where laughs abound.

Earthworms wiggle in a race,
While the flowers blush, a lovely face.
Fungi giggle, sprouting tall,
As mushrooms gather, having a ball.

The roots below start to chuckle loud,
For nature's comedy should be a crowd!
Join in the joy, be part of this cheer,
As the rooted realm holds humor dear.

The Quiet Chorus of the Lowlands

In lowlands where the sunflowers sway,
Grasshoppers leap in their ballet.
A turtle grins, slow but sly,
While daisies gossip, oh my my!

Down by the stream, a frog sings loud,
As dragonflies join, sweet and proud.
A rabbit chuckles, munching grass,
Saying, "Who needs to hurry past?"

The willows shake, their leaves delight,
Whispering tales through day and night.
A bat swoops down, in a funny spree,
Doing somersaults with glee.

This quiet chorus, a playful sound,
In the lowlands where joy is found.
So when you stroll and hear the cheer,
Know humor lives all around here.

The Fable of Ferns

In a forest of green, where the ferns like to giggle,
A squirrel with a hat, oh how he did wiggle.
He danced on the leaves, with moves so bizarre,
While birds in the branches applauded from afar.

The mushrooms were laughing, tops wobbling with glee,
As the raccoon joined in, what a sight to see!
He tried to jump high, but tripped on a vine,
Landed right in mud, oh, how he did whine!

The wise old oak chuckled, with bark full of tales,
Of creatures who frolicked and dodged through the gales.
They whispered fun secrets, shared tricks of the trade,
In a world of pure jest, where no one was afraid.

So come laugh with the ferns, in this playful domain,
Where mischief runs wild, and joy is the main.
For nature is silly, in all its grand schemes,
In the whimsical world, where even mud dreams.

Monologues of the Murky Bed

In the depths of the creek, where the tadpoles conspire,
A frog wore a bowtie, said, 'I'm quite the sire!'
He croaked out a joke, made the minnows all cringe,
But laughter erupted, and the waters did sing.

A snail, very slow, took the stage for a rhyme,
Said, 'I carry my house, that's thrift, not a crime!'
The fish rolled their eyes, but they couldn't resist,
As the chorus of frogs joined in, none could be missed.

Then up popped a turtle, slow as can be,
He said with a wink, 'I'm the star, can't you see?'
He shared a weird fact, then gave quite the grin,
'Toc-toc,' said the muskrat, 'You're a laugh with that chin!'

In the sludge and the muck, where the antics flow free,
Life's funny and quirky, come join the spree.
Each ripple a giggle, each splash a delight,
In the murky abode, where the jokes shine so bright.

The Timid Notes from the Understory

In the shadiest nook, where the shadows play tricks,
A beetle with glasses read poems to the ticks.
With a stutter he spoke, and they gathered quite round,
Not knowing that soon, they'd all fall to the ground.

A shy little mouse whispered tales with a squeak,
Of the weird things he'd seen, like a crab in a creek.
He fumbled his words, oh, how silly he felt,
But the laughter erupted—what a twist the tale dealt!

Then came a young lizard, who, nervous, turned red,
He forgot all his lines, and just danced instead.
With each silly wiggle, the audience roared,
In the undergrowth's light, where humor was stored.

So listen for whispers, beneath leafy domains,
Where critters like jesters play funny old games.
In the depths of the woods, where the timid unite,
Laughter's a treasure that sparks pure delight.

The Sones of Subterranean Life

Beneath the thick soil, where the secrets reside,
A mole with a flute tried to dance and abide.
Each note that he played made the earthworms all sway,
In a concert of giggles that brightened the day.

A gopher chimed in with a rafter of cheer,
He tapped on the ground, 'Let's make music down here!'
With rhythms of roots, they tapped, clapped, and hummed,
As the moles in the shadows felt joy overcome.

Then came the bold badger, with moves on full blast,
He spun with a flourish, a dance unsurpassed.
But his tail got stuck in a burrow so deep,
And the laughter erupted, from fissures they'd weep!

The notes from below, they echoed with joy,
In the world of the earthy, each critter, a toy.
So dig deep for the laughter that bubbles and flows,
In the songs of the soil, where the humor just grows.

Caresses of the Woodland Whisper

In the woods, a squirrel jumps high,
Chasing dreams beneath the sky.
Fuzzy nuts are on his mind,
He giggles, quite unrefined.

The trees gossip in leafy tones,
While ants parade like tiny drones.
A rabbit wears a cap of grass,
Dancing while the moments pass.

Raccoons leer from hidden spots,
Sniffing out the tastiest plots.
With every rustle, joy takes flight,
The woodland's glee is pure delight.

And though the owl pretends to frown,
Even he can't dampen the crown.
For in this realm of leafy cheer,
Laughter echoes, loud and clear.

Secrets in the Shade

Beneath the leaves, a party brews,
With bouncing bugs in vibrant hues.
A worm does the cha-cha, feet so small,
While toads play cards and have a ball.

The sun sneaks in, just a grin,
As butterflies stretch their soft, thin skin.
A hedgehog juggles acorns with ease,
Next to him, a fox, a tease!

Whispers swirl beneath the boughs,
"Who took the pie?" a goat endows.
The answer's lost in giggles bright,
While shadows dance in sheer delight.

In this glade, odd friendships grow,
As mischievous winds begin to blow.
Secrets bubble in every shade,
Where laughter weaves a lovely braid.

Sighs of the Shaded Realm

In the glen where shadows prance,
A tortoise joins a bustling dance.
His moves are slow, but full of flair,
While fireflies buzz, lighting the air.

The whispers tickle the ferns so neat,
As hedgehogs race on tiny feet.
They trip and tumble, what a sight,
In this shaded realm, pure delight!

A wise old tree gives sage advice,
"Don't take life too cold or nice!"
Squirrels laugh, they mock and tease,
"Hey there, old trunk! Just chill and ease!"

Among the crooks where shadows lay,
Each critter finds a way to play.
With laughter echoing through the green,
It's the silliest party ever seen.

The Grasp of Green Imagery

Amidst the vines where ferns are vast,
A frog recites verses quite fast.
Reciting tales of knights and cheese,
While critters chuckle with ease.

A breeze arrives, oh what a tease,
It tousles tails, shakes golden leaves.
A badger joins the flowy fun,
Rolling along, he's second to none.

Rabbits giggle at all the fuss,
As sunlight fills the leafy bus.
They hop and bounce, so light and free,
Making art of every spree!

In this lovely green embrace,
Nature spins a funny space.
Every creature knows the game,
In this realm of joy and fame.

The Breath of the Verdant Shadows

In shady spots where critters play,
A squirrel steals a snack all day.
The trees all giggle in the breeze,
While ants march by, too busy to freeze.

Bright mushrooms pop like tiny hats,
As lazy beetles do their chats.
A snail slips by with elegance rare,
While rabbits hop, without a care.

The vines all wriggle, oh what a dance!
They beckon to frogs to join the prance.
And if you listen with your heart,
You'll hear the whispers of nature's art.

In every shade, a jest unfolds,
As secrets in the green woods hold.
So laugh along with roots and leaves,
For life's a game, or so it seems!

Secrets Wrapped in Silence

Underneath the leafy throne,
A hedgehog curls as if alone.
But listen close, and you will find,
The gossip of the forest unlined.

The rabbits joke in softest tones,
While owls pretended they were stones.
A dance of shadows plays on ground,
As whispers tickle all around.

The hidden tales of twisted roots,
Speak volumes of their silly hoots.
An acorn drops with a thud and roll,
Laughs echo from the oldest soul.

So come, dear friend, and share a laugh,
Nature's comedy, a flowing path.
In every rustle, you will see,
Life's a jest in the green, carefree!

Threads of Life Intertwined

In tangled greens, the stories flow,
Of caterpillars putting on a show.
They wear their stripes with big delight,
Wiggling round in sweet moonlight.

While ladybugs debate the best,
On where to settle, what a jest!
Grasshoppers leap, and frogs will croak,
In a chorus of joy, a cheerful stroke.

The dandelions spread their wishes wide,
While tiny ants take life in stride.
Together in chaos, they find their tune,
As fireflies blink, they swoon and croon.

Life's threads entwine in jest, you see,
Each creature winks in harmony.
In this wild weave, let laughter rise,
For Mother Nature wears her disguise!

The Breath of the Forest Floor

Beneath the trees, a carpet lies,
Of whispers sweet and silly sighs.
Where critters dance with carefree glee,
And roots play tag without a fee.

Mossy beds hide giggling sprites,
While crickets serenade the nights.
A turtle thinks he's quite the ace,
As he strolls at a leisurely pace.

The mushrooms giggle when raindrops fall,
As droplet races make a call.
And when the sun peeks through so bright,
The forest glimmers with pure delight.

So take a stroll on this wild shore,
Where laughter blooms and spirits soar.
In every nook, there's joy to explore,
Among the tales of the forest floor!

Shrouded in Green Silence

In the forest, whispers roam,
Leaves giggle as they build a home.
Snails wear hats, oh what a sight,
Pinecones chuckle, it's their night!

Mushrooms dance with wiggly glee,
Squirrels tell tales, wild and free.
A hedgehog jokes about a fight,
With a sleeping bug, who snores too tight.

Crickets chirp in secret code,
While the toads hop down the road.
The breeze tickles branches, they shake and sway,
A party unfolds in leafy ballet.

Beneath the ferns, laughter does spread,
As beetles share rumors, chattering in bed.
With acorns clapping, the night will roll,
For in this greenery, it's all a jesting soul!

Sylvan Secrets Unveiled

Beneath the trees, a jolly scene,
Where raccoons wear masks, feeling quite keen.
A fox tells jokes with a winking eye,
As owls hoot laughter, oh my, oh my!

Worms gossip low about the day,
While whispers linger in a playful array.
Bouncing bunnies hop to a tune,
While fireflies twinkle, a sparkly swoon.

Caterpillars knit in a silly style,
Creating scarves that go for a mile.
Fungi giggle and wiggle with glee,
Making all critters feel jubilant and free.

A squirrel's acorn falls with a thud,
And the chatter grows louder, a riotous flood.
In this hidden land where secrets thrive,
Nature's comedy keeps the laughter alive!

Hushed Tales from the Underbrush

In the shade, whispers converse,
With the green leaves in a funny verse.
A beetle jokes, "I'm late for lunch!"
While ants march in for a buffet brunch.

Bamboo sways with a giggling sway,
"Don't tickle me, or I'll dance away!"
With spiders weaving comedic webs,
They catch tiny laughs, not just tiny insects.

Chipmunks chatter, full of zest,
Trading puns; they're simply the best!
Grasshoppers bounce with timing precise,
Making each leap feel like a dice.

A badger joins in, a storyteller true,
With each tall tale, something funny ensues.
In this cozy nook, all creatures convene,
Sharing giggles, oh what a scene!

The Language of the Undergrowth

In the thicket, secrets unfold,
With critters clever and stories bold.
A lizard croons with a silly flair,
While the moss chuckles, hiding its hair.

The thrum of nature, a playful hum,
As mushrooms plot a dance, oh so fun!
With raccoons spinning in a grove,
Each move they make, a funny trove.

Cockroaches gossip about a cat,
Saying, "Do you remember that?"
With grass blades nodding in jestful glee,
They keep the punchlines light and free.

A tortoise grins, "I'm speeding today,"
With a wink that drives birds to play.
In the dense foliage, joy does arise,
A comedy club beneath open skies.

The Enchantment of the Emerald Floor

A carpet green, beneath our feet,
Where tiny elves dance to their beat.
They giggle and tumble, quite the sight,
In the dappled sun, such pure delight.

A worm in a tux, oh what a sight!
He twirls around, a dance in the light.
With twigs as swords, they play their game,
In this leafy realm, they seek their fame.

Frogs in bow ties croak their tune,
While ants form lines, a tiny commune.
The breeze whispers jokes, makes us laugh,
In this emerald wonder, nature's photograph.

Their antics are wild, a comical spree,
The forest floor, a sight to see!
With every step, joy's footprint found,
In a world where silly knows no bound.

Threads of Life in the Leafy Deep

In tangled vines, we weave our fate,
A sloth on a thread, but oh, how late!
He dreams of racing, fast as a hare,
Yet naps through the day without a care.

A squirrel rehearses his stand-up show,
With banana peels, he steals the glow.
His audience—bugs, their laughter loud,
In leafy depths, they gather proud.

A raccoon with glasses reads a tome,
Naming acorns, feeling right at home.
While mushrooms giggle, wearing their caps,
Oh, the humor in innocence, plenty of laughs!

The threads that bind us may twist and twine,
In this quirky forest, all's just fine.
Each blooper and blunder, a tale to share,
In the leafy deep, there's joy everywhere.

The Stillness of Soggy Soil

In the gooey mud, we all shall tread,
With squishy squeaks, it's comedy bred.
A snail in a race, still taking its time,
Looking so proud, like it's in its prime.

The puddles chuckle, a watery laugh,
As frogs practice jumps, on their little path.
They trip on their tongues, oh what a jest,
In wetlands of joy, they're truly blessed.

A toad in a top hat gives a grand speech,
To the critters all gathered, a lesson to teach.
"Don't rush!" he croaks, "life's a slow thrill,"
As a duck slides by, with absolute will.

Soggy soil holds mischief and glee,
With every squelch, there's jubilee.
In this damp haven, we roll and play,
United in laughter, come join the fray!

Murmured Legends of the Forest Floor

In whispers of leaves, tales are spun,
Of a brave little mouse who dared to run.
He chased a shadow, then lost his way,
In search of adventure, a comical play.

The beetles debate whose carapace shines,
While ants craft a train with flexible lines.
They march in circles, quite dizzy by noon,
"Oh where's the exit?" they hum a tune.

A brave little snail sings, "I'm slow but proud!"
As butterflies giggle, lost in the crowd.
With bows in their wings, they flutter and flit,
Admiring the snail, while he tries to quit.

Legends are forged, silly and bold,
In a tapestry woven of laughter untold.
On the forest floor, with whimsy we roam,
Creating our stories, forever our home.

www.ingramcontent.com/pod-product-compliance
Lightning Source LLC
Chambersburg PA
CBHW071821160426
43209CB00003B/160